little book of

NEW YORK
style

Kristen Bateman is a New York City-based writer, editor and creative consultant who specializes in fashion, beauty and culture. She regularly writes for the *New York Times* Style Section, *Vogue*, *Harper's Bazaar*, *Town & Country*, *Architectural Digest*, *Elle*, and many other magazines. Her focus is on writing about fashion history, culture and beauty. She also has her own jewelry brand, Dollchunk.

Published in 2023 by Welbeck
An imprint of Welbeck Non-Fiction Limited,
part of Welbeck Publishing Group.
Offices in: London – 20 Mortimer Street, London W1T 3JW &
Sydney – 205 Commonwealth Street, Surry Hills 2010
www.welbeckpublishing.com

ISBN 978-1-80279-490-8

Printed in China

10 9 8 7 6 5 4 3 2

KRISTEN BATEMAN

little book of

NEW YORK style

WELBECK

CONTENTS

iNTRODUCTiON

New York style is the most indescribable and exhilarating concept. Among all the fashion capitals in the world, New York is one place where you can pretty much wear whatever you want and not get any strange looks. Cities like Paris and London have their own style signatures built up over the course of decades that are immediately recognizable, not just for their aesthetic and their intrinsic meaning – but New York style is more of an amalgamation of everything under the sun (and moon) with a heavy dose of never-ending excitement of what's to come.

Sure, there are certain stereotypes about New York and its fashion. Take, for example, the cliché of dressing all in black or carrying multiple bags on the subway to stash a pair of shoes, a laptop and everything else in your life. I've done both at different points in my life, for different reasons. But behind these tropes, there is so much history.

New York has always stood as the capital of American style, and that's not just because the city stands as a cultural beacon. For decades, it was the centre of clothing manufacturing for the United States.

The Garment District officially took shape in 1919, but even before that, New York City was the hub for clothing. The uniforms needed by the Union Army during the Civil War

Opposite: A model walking the runway, wearing Samuel Winston, at one of the earliest New York Fashion Weeks, 1953.

Overleaf: Workers in the Garment District pulling racks of clothing, 1955.

A scene from a factory in the Garment District in the 1950s.

in the 1860s called for mass production, which was possible here, and by 1910, the garment industry made up almost half of the industrial labour force in the city. The vast majority of those workers were immigrants, including a huge population of Jewish descendants from Europe. Hundreds of thousands of them came to work here and by 1926, the Garment District was growing faster than any other area in the entire city. During the Second World War, the Nazi occupation of Paris inspired the industry, the Garment Workers' Union, and Mayor LaGuardia to create the New York Dress Institute and promote New York as the fashion capital of the world: "New York Creation" labels, depicting an iconic New York skyscraper, were stitched into pieces.

It was in the 1940s that many of the New York fashion signatures which we know today came to fruition. New York Fashion Week, for example, was established in 1943 by publicist Eleanor Lambert, then known as "press week". The idea was to hold the event in a centralized location (then, the Plaza Hotel) and invite press from New York and across the United States to see the work of American designers like Claire McCardell, Hattie Carnegie and Norman Norell.

New York Fashion Week is still instantly recognizable, even as other historical aspects of New York's fashion DNA, like the Garment District, have faded over the years. But if there's one thing you can expect from the lexicon of stylish New Yorkers, it's intrinsic self-expression through their wardrobes. Every piece they select is precisely planned, whether that's a pristinely designed T-shirt from The Row (the luxury brand created by honorary New Yorkers Mary-Kate and Ashley Olsen) or a New York Yankees baseball cap. With that, New Yorkers write the history and future of the city's fashion as they walk through the streets, wait on subway platforms and go about their business.

Introduction

chapter 1

WHAT IS NEW YORK STYLE?

Attempting to define New York style is no small feat, and that's because New York City is the most diverse city in the world. Walk down any street in any neighbourhood and you'll hear a plethora of different languages, just as you'll see so many different aesthetics reflected and refracted back at you. The idea that anything goes here is almost intrinsic.

Unlike other parts of the country which are often more conservative or follow certain rules, New York lacks structure in its style DNA. The blend of cultures from all over the world, as well as the high numbers of people in the city who are just visiting, makes for the most varied mix you'll likely ever see. One of the most comical things about being a fashion-loving New Yorker is that you can always tell who's a tourist: they dress a little bit more casually than the rest of us.

Scroll through any photo round-up from New York Fashion Week and you can bet it's more colourful, expressive and diverse than any other fashion capital in the world. "Everything in fashion begins in the street," the fashion designer Diane von Furstenberg once said. One of the most famous street style photographers, who made history as the go-to source for the evolution of New York style, was Bill Cunningham. Beginning his career as a milliner, he also worked at a dress shop in Manhattan, with clients ranging from Marilyn Monroe to Katharine Hepburn. He ended up befriending Jacqueline Kennedy after she came in to request help dyeing a red suit to black for the funeral of her husband, John F. Kennedy.

Inspired by his high society friends, Cunningham originally started writing about fashion for *Women's Wear Daily* and the *Chicago Tribune*, and in the late 1970s began snapping candid

Sarah Jessica Parker as Carrie Bradshaw of *Sex and the City* wearing her iconic tutu in the show's intro.

photos of New Yorkers and what they wore in their everyday life for the *New York Times*.

His 1978 picture of the actress Greta Garbo was considered his big break, though he himself wasn't even aware that it was the reclusive actress: he had been captivated by her coat. Up until his death in 2016, Cunningham showed the plurality of the New Yorker: the eccentricity, the severity, the low-fi casual. The photos he often took were of unsuspecting New Yorkers, in the rain or on the way to work: "You see how people really live and how they really dress," he once said. That same kind of sentiment can still be seen today when looking at New York fashion and how the everyday mundane shapes it. It's fluid, it's moving and it's ever-changing, perennially adapting to its surroundings and culture.

Still, there are clichés that can prove to be true. If you go to parts of the Upper East Side on a Sunday, for instance, you're likely to see more people with expensive handbags and conservatively cut clothes. If you go to Soho on a Saturday, you're more likely to see a younger crowd that's dressed up in a mix of emerging designer pieces, current season designers, rare vintage and fast fashion. Certain areas of the city at certain times are definitely more centred on peacocking and dressing up.

Still, New York might be one of the few places on earth where you can never feel overdressed. You could walk down the street to get coffee in a ballgown, and some people wouldn't bat an eye. Or you could wear sweatpants to Fashion Week. Truly, anything goes, but what unites it all is the value of independence and choosing what you want to wear for your own sake. In New York, there's never one overwhelming

What Is New York Style?

Bill Cunningham, the legendary photographer of New York street style.

The front row at a show during New York Fashion Week.

trend, shape, silhouette or brand – because the taste levels are so varied. Instead, there's a sort of disregard for trends and more of a focus on the independence of dress. It's about authenticity but it's also about freedom.

But back to those clichés: does the everyday New Yorker wear all black? Take the subway and you'll see that a good amount of them do. This is because it creates an easy, sleek look that offers an unbothered sensibility while also conveying power and stature at the same time. Coco Chanel famously created her innovative little black dress as we know it in the 1920s, but the symbol of black clothing and what it means would be further reinvented when Audrey Hepburn wore a little black dress designed by Hubert de Givenchy during the opening scene of *Breakfast at Tiffany's* in 1961.

Undoubtedly, movies and TV throughout the ages have served as cultural signifiers of what New York style is too. In 1954, Marilyn Monroe famously wore a white pleated dress by costume designer William Travilla in *The Seven Year Itch*, as the wind billowed and blew her dress up above the subway grate. The look was one that represented the iconic bombshell and femme fatale – plus the flashiness of New York – with its plunging neckline and halter design. The scene was originally filmed on Lexington Avenue (but would later have to be reshot in a studio due to the chaos caused by onlookers).

There are certain TV shows that put a specific kind of New York aesthetic on display, shaping and dictating it for the entire world, whether real or fantasy. Sarah Jessica Parker as Carrie Bradshaw is one of the most iconic examples of New York style to be broadcast across America and the world for years. The actress starred as the fashionable columnist in the TV series *Sex and the City* as well as the movies that followed and the reboot, *And Just Like That*. In the original series and movies, she was styled by the prolific New York stylist Patricia Field. Her most famous outfit is the sheer pink, barely there tank top styled with heels and a white tutu, sourced by Field for $5 from a costume showroom. But she also wore out-there cowboy hats, John Galliano's famed newspaper dress from Dior's Autumn/Winter 2000 show and other pieces directly from the runway: Vivienne Westwood satin miniskirts with bustles, Prada striped skirts, and DKNY slips. It was the first time that high fashion was seen in such a capacity on TV, and it put New York on the map as a global fashion capital.

Likewise, other TV shows put the idea of New York as a fashion capital to work. *Gossip Girl* was styled by Eric Daman, who worked under Patricia Field on *Sex and the City*, and who took inspiration from the actual style tribes he saw on the Upper East Side. Daman would hang out near schools – specifically, private schools – and look out for stylish outfits, which inspired the different characters' wardrobes on the show. Prep was reinvented by Blair Waldorf, boho was reinterpreted by Serena van der Woodsen and emo punk was riffed on by Jenny Humphrey. Beyond *Sex and the City*, *Gossip Girl* was the only other show that showcased the variety of fashion and its various aesthetics in New York.

In 2021, *Gossip Girl*, like *Sex and the City*, staged a reboot. Pegged as an extension and a standalone sequel to the original series, the new *Gossip Girl* said an equal amount about New York style. Daman was brought on to style the show yet again, but this time he took a much more casual approach. For the most part, the characters' wardrobes in the show are void of bright colours and identifying accessories. Instead, the looks are more inspired by casualwear and athleisure, and the fashion is more blurred in terms of gender lines. Girls wear boxy silhouettes and oversized button-downs while the guys don sweatshirts and casual separates. Daman put a focus on emerging designers like Christopher John Rogers, known for his decadent dresses spun in vibrant colours and illuminating prints. All these efforts signify recent changes in the shifting New York fashion landscape.

Right top: The original cast of *Gossip Girl*, which ran from 2007 to 2012.

Right below: The cast of the sequel *Gossip Girl*, 2021.

Overleaf: A model walks the runway in a signature voluminous dress by Christopher John Rogers.

On the other hand, there have been shows that have taken on the idea of New York style from a different angle. Take, for example, *The Nanny*, the 1990s sitcom in which Fran Fine works as a live-in nanny for a Broadway producer's three children. Hailing from Queens, she has an aesthetic that is loud and bold. The show's stylist, Brenda Cooper, won an Emmy for her work, and styled Drescher in colourful Moschino blazers, fur-trimmed coats and plenty of kitschy skirt suits covered in polka dots or chequerboard prints, or rendered in green tweed or orange leather.

There's a certain history of celebrity, too, which has made New York style particularly unique. Unlike L.A., or even London, New York style is more personality-driven and less about following one archetype. When Mary-Kate and Ashley Olsen attended NYU for instance, they defined an aesthetic generationally with their oversized looks, slouchy bags, little to no makeup and dark colour palette. Whereas London celebrities might follow conventions to look more polished, or those in L.A. might make sure they have perfect make-up and hair and wear clothes that show off more skin, you can truly be whoever you want to be in New York. There's no such thing as fitting into one box.

There's also something to say about the fact that New Yorkers have a habit of becoming accidental style icons in their own right. Jennifer Lopez, for example, may be one of the most famous New Yorkers of all time. She grew up in the Bronx and started out as a dancer before turning to acting and singing. Working her way up to become the first Hispanic actress to earn more than $1 million for a movie, she also changed the face of fashion as a New Yorker.

Fran Drescher as *The Nanny*, who often wore geometric, kitschy pieces in the TV series.

"Fashion is a scale here, and taste is a spectrum. Either way, you'll create your own narrative."

Lopez wore a tropical green Versace silk chiffon dress to the 42nd Grammy Awards ceremony on 23 February 2000 – and shocked the world with the extremely low-cut neckline that plunged below her belly button. In fact, this very moment was what led to the creation of Google Image Search. "People wanted more than just text. This first became apparent after the 2000 Grammy Awards, where Jennifer Lopez wore a green dress that, well, caught the world's attention," former Google CEO and executive chairman Eric Schmidt wrote on Project Syndicate in 2015. "At the time, it was the most popular search query we had ever seen. But we had no surefire way of getting users exactly what they wanted: JLo wearing that dress. Google Image Search was born."

As the idea of American fashion shifts throughout history, New York continues to offer up a safe haven for individuality. You can do what you want here. You can care a lot, or not at all! What's profound is that both make a statement, and someone will probably admire your look in some way, no matter what you wear. Fashion is a scale here, and taste is a spectrum. Either way, you'll create your own narrative.

New Yorker Jennifer Lopez in the Versace dress credited for inspiring the invention of Google Images.

chapter 2

THE ORIGINALS

The designer icons of New York fashion made their power moves in the 1920s. They began striking out on their own, making names for themselves in New York City with their own brands, rather than taking their major inspiration from their European counterparts, as they had done in the past. The fashion industry as we know it really began in the 1850s with the establishment of fashion houses that brought fame to individual designers. Charles Frederick Worth, an English designer based in Paris, was one of the first to sew his label into his clothing, hosted fashion shows and formed the modern-day couture house (which exists, albeit in different forms, to this day).

But New York designers did things their own way. Born in Maryland in 1905, Claire McCardell remains one of the most iconic New York City designers of all time. In the 1920s, she studied at the famous Parsons School of Design, first in New York and then at its location in Paris, where she combed the city's flea markets to find couture samples that she would take apart to learn from the stitching. In 1932, she began working for the designer Robert Turk, who took her with him in 1932 to join Townley Frocks, Inc. Turk passed away in a tragic accident and McCardell was forced to take over the business and show her own collection. She explained later that she created it by doing what many designers of the time were doing: copying Paris.

But the DNA of New York fashion was really turned on its head when McCardell started experimenting with her own

New York Designers

A model wearing a colourful design by Claire McCardell.

Above: A tailored Claire McCardell dress,
photographed by Horst P. Horst, 1949.

Opposite: A grey-striped wool jersey dinner
dress, by Claire McCardell, 1946.

intrinsically casual sportswear. In 1938, she introduced the "Monastic Dress", a loose-hanging, comfortable dress cut on the bias. A buyer from Manhattan's Best and Company ordered 100 of the dresses, which sold out. Imitations flooded the market – the first time in modern history that other American designers were copying a New York designer instead of one from Europe. The Second World War led to rationing and severe shortages of material, and McCardell proved resourceful. That, combined with her ability to focus on the ease which American women demanded, made her the star of the New York fashion scene. Her clothing was less structured and free of shoulder pads as well as affordable and versatile, ensuring that pieces could be mixed and matched – a benefit that became a selling point, featured in advertising. A 1955 *Time* magazine article described her work as: "dresses that are as at home in the front seat of a station wagon as in the back seat of a Rolls, as comfortable in the vestibule of a motel as in the lobby of the Waldorf, as fitting for work in the office as for cocktails and dinner with the boss." She also included details usually associated with men's work clothes: blue-jean topstitching, trouser pleats, and pockets. Her "Popover" dress was designed for the wartime housewife who wanted something that could be worn both casually and for entertaining.

McCardell's peers, including Norman Norell, took inspiration from the same ease and casual aesthetic of American fashion that would shape and define New York's style identity. Norell, after all, was presented with the first Coty American Fashion Critics Award in 1943 by the Mayor of New York City, Fiorello LaGuardia. He was also the first American designer to have his own name on a dress label. He studied at Parsons School of Design, like McCardell and started his work in the early 1920s, as

One of Norman Norell's sequined dresses, 1971.

Above: A model wearing a Hattie Carnegie look, 1941.

Opposite: Another mermaid gown, for which designer
Norman Norell became famous.

a costume designer for Paramount Pictures. Later he worked with Anthony Traina to design their Traina-Norell label, founded in 1941. He had a keen eye for minimalism with a splash of New York glamour. In response to fabric rationing, he created slim versions of dropped-waist chemise dresses, in the style of 1920s flappers. He was also the first to do leopard print on a large scale, and his attention to detail and luxury was what attracted high society women and A-list celebrities like Marilyn Monroe. One of his most memorable designs was the "mermaid dress", a floor-length silk gown encrusted with thousands of shimmering hand-sewn sequins. It reportedly took 250 hours to create each gown. "In the evening you have to knock 'em dead with glitter," he explained.

Both McCardell and Norell spent time working with another designer who would come to shape New York fashion: Hattie Carnegie. Born in Vienna in 1886 as Henrietta Kanengeiser, she changed her surname to Carnegie when she was in her twenties as an homage to Andrew Carnegie, the richest person in the United States at the time. Her family emigrated to New York City's Lower East Side – once a major hub for garment production in New York – when Hattie was a child. She started working at Macy's at age 13, modelled and trimmed hats at a milliner at 15, and by 1909 she created a hat-making business with Rose Roth, taking control of the business in 1919.

Carnegie began buying dresses from Paris, using them for inspiration for her own pieces. These were designed by the industry's top talent, including Norell, McCardell, Jean Louis and Pauline Trigère. That was how Carnegie made her name: she famously couldn't sew but had an eye for what, or rather, who, was going to be the next big thing. In 1928, Lucille Ball, then largely unknown, was scouted by Carnegie to work as her in-house model. Ball said, "Hattie taught me how to

Designer Hattie Carnegie photographed with her dog.

slouch properly in a $1,000 hand-sewn sequin dress and how to wear a $40,000 sable coat as casually as rabbit." By 1929, her sales had reached $3.5 million per year and her business eventually grew to a value of $8 million per year – all run out of her East Forty-Ninth Street store in Manhattan until her death in 1956. Her signature was the "Little Carnegie suit," a jacket with a severe waist, and a skirt with rounded hips.

Carnegie was also one of the first New York designers to create an empire, complete with cosmetics, perfumes and accessories.

New York Designers

MiD-CENTURY iCONS

By the 1950s, the European designers that New Yorkers once mimicked were starting to look to the Americans for inspiration. One such New York designer to make major waves was Ann Lowe, who was admired by Christian Dior himself. Originally from Alabama, Lowe established her business there but moved to Harlem in the 1930s and set up her shops around the Upper East Side of Manhattan. She is famously referred to as the first Black woman to become a noted fashion designer, and designed the ivory silk taffeta wedding dress worn by Jacqueline Bouvier when she married John F. Kennedy in 1953.

Lowe specialized in evening and bridalwear and sold her pieces around the country in upscale department stores. She had couture-like salons, where customers could shop and be fitted, at a few locations on Madison Avenue. At the height of her business in the 1950s, she said she sold a thousand gowns per year.

At the onset of the 1960s, New York had already established itself as a global destination for celebrity fashion, custom luxury, expert craftsmanship and sportswear. What was new in the mix, however, was the appeal of youth culture. New York pushed the concept of the boutique and what it could be. Take, for example, the store Paraphernalia, which

New York Designers

Ann Lowe adjusting a gown in 1962, worn by Alice Baker.

"The European designers that New Yorkers once mimicked were starting to look to the Americans for inspiration."

opened on the corner of 67th Street and Madison Avenue, by the British entrepreneur Paul Young. It was a major contrast to other retailers of the time. While the department stores Lord & Taylor, Bergdorf Goodman, and Bonwit Teller took a conservative approach, Paraphernalia had a retro futuristic design by modernist architect Ulrich Franzen, a go-go dancing girl in the window and the freshest and most shocking designs, like the miniskirt, from the coolest and newest designers. He hired up-and-coming talent, like Betsey Johnson, to create otherworldly clothing out of paper, cardboard, plastic and vinyl, and all pieces cost under $100. Jean Shrimpton, Andy Warhol, the Velvet Underground and Edie Sedgwick could often be found hanging out in the store. Johnson would go on to be a major influence of the fashion industry – as she is to this day. By the end of 1968, there were four Paraphernalia stores in Manhattan, one in Southampton, New York, and 44 total across the United States, but by the late 1970s, each of them had closed their doors.

An ivory gown decorated with blooming handmade fabric rose vines, designed by Ann Lowe, 1966–1967.

New York Designers

DiSCO DESiGNERS

The 1970s in New York were marked by an explosion of fashion brands led by designers who took inspiration from their predecessors. The same casual, cool elements of American sportswear, which really started in the 1940s, now came in the form of Calvin Klein's denim, Ralph Lauren's Americana-influenced pieces, Halston's fluid jersey dresses, and Diane von Furstenberg's wrap dresses.

New York's club scene was also opening up at the time, and places like Studio 54 influenced the clothes that every aspirational New Yorker wanted to wear. Diana Ross, Bianca and Mick Jagger, Farrah Fawcett, Donna Summer, Elton John, Liza Minnelli, Grace Jones, Jerry Hall and Debbie Harry could be found on the stage as well as on the dance floor as they mingled with some of the top designers of the time, like Halston and von Furstenberg. It was around this time that New York designers mixed with celebrities and became household names themselves. Studio 54 would close in 1980, but not before it had defined an era of decadent glamour, opulence and excess. As the 1980s approached, designers started turning towards a cleaner and more casual aesthetic that felt new.

Perhaps no name is more synonymous with New York fashion in the 1980s than Donna Karan. In contrast to the big shoulders, power suits, all-black and monied Wall Street look

New York Designers

Designer Roy Halston Frowick, better known simply as Halston, with one of his models in his studio.

Above: Halston and his muses wearing the
designer's signature jersey pieces, 1972.

Opposite: Designer Diane von Furstenberg
pictured in the 1970s.

Above: Designer Donna Karan and Louis Dell'Olio in Anne Klein's workroom in the Garment District, 1980.

Opposite: Model and actress Lisa Taylor wearing Ralph Lauren, 1976.

also happening at the time in Manhattan, Karan offered up a new vision. She studied at Parsons School of Design, and later worked under designer Anne Klein, launching her namesake collection in 1985. Her "Essentials" line offered seven easy pieces, versatile, flexible wardrobe staples that emanated an effortlessly stylish vibe. The bodysuit, a skirt, a pair of pants, a tailored jacket, a cashmere sweater, a white shirt and tights were the original pieces that built her brand.

New York Designers

THE NEW 90S

The 1990s would mark a new level of organization of New York fashion designers. The schedule and system of New York Fashion Week (NYFW) had been largely unchanged since it was founded in the 1940s by Eleanor Lambert. The industry's biggest names, like Anna Sui, Betsey Johnson and Ralph Lauren, were showing across the city in all different locations. When part of the ceiling fell on fashion critic Suzy Menkes's head at a Michael Kors show in 1991, Fern Mallis – then executive director of the CFDA – decided that NYFW needed a new direction and a central location. Bryant Park was chosen as the hub for most of the 1990s until the mid 2010s. Fashion Week later moved to Lincoln Center, where it would stay for a few years, before decentralizing again, as it is today.

Yet the 1990s is really when New York Fashion began to strike a new path. New York became the place for innovation, new ideas and rule breakers. Anna Sui and Betsey Johnson had fantastical shows with fully fledged sets – from beauty parlours to forests – and all the top models, from Naomi Campbell to Linda Evangelista, and even non-fashion celebrities like Dave Navarro of the Red Hot Chili Peppers walking in shows. Marc Jacobs presented his infamous Spring 1993 show for Perry Ellis, which shocked the industry with its take on grunge, the subculture that took its inspiration directly from the streets. Celebrities were ever-present, like Julia Roberts, Leonardo DiCaprio, Drew Barrymore and Mariah Carey. Edgy labels like Helmut Lang and Alexander McQueen also chose New York as the place to present their shows, over the other big fashion capitals like London, Milan and Paris.

New York Designers

Naomi Campbell walking Anna Sui's Spring/Summer 1994 runway show.

Model Stella Tennant photographed by Arthur Elgort for *Vogue*, October 1995.

Model Christy Turlington walking in a 90s show for Calvin Klein.

New York Designers

A scene from Betsey Johnson's Spring/Summer 1994 show.

THE NEXT GENERATION

Today, many of the designers who made innovative strides are still mainstays of the New York fashion industry, like Marc Jacobs, Diane von Furstenberg and Ralph Lauren, to name a few.

But what makes New York's designers today feel especially interesting is the new and diverse talent from all over the world. Where in the past New York Fashion Week had become known for big powerhouse names that dominated for decades, the 2020s really marked an exploration of new designers to know, and the city has welcomed them with open arms.

New brands are establishing their businesses in New York City every day, each with their own aesthetics and each with a determination to create their own vision and unique point of view in the industry. Eckhaus Latta, for example, is an American fashion label established in 2011 by Mike Eckhaus and Zoe Latta, which has become now iconic for its frayed knits, off-kilter denim and textural dresses. It was the first fashion brand to have an exhibition at the Whitney Museum in 2018.

New York Designers

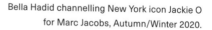

Bella Hadid channelling New York icon Jackie O
for Marc Jacobs, Autumn/Winter 2020.

Above: Zoe Latta and Mike Eckhaus, the designers behind Eckhaus Latta.

Opposite: A shimmering look from Eckhaus Latta's Autumn/
Winter 2022 collection, presented on the Lower East Side.

"Brands are redefining what New York fashion means and how it can be reinterpreted."

Pyer Moss was founded in 2013 by Kerby Jean-Raymond, and has become another favourite. Jean-Raymond describes the brand as an "art project" or "a timely social experiment" and often produces performance-like shows that hint at social commentary. It was the first brand led by a Black American man to be on the official Paris Haute Couture Fashion Week schedule in 2021.

This and other brands, such as Thom Browne, founded in 2001 as a line of made-to-measure menswear, are redefining what New York fashion means and how it can be reinterpreted through the lens of the New Yorker – whether that means a keen eye on inverted prep staples or an indelible take on dressed up tailoring.

New York Designers

Looks from Pyer Moss, which capture the unique approach of designer Kerby Jean-Raymond, who creates couture-like sportswear.

Above: Broadway producer Jordan Roth who modelled in
Thom Browne's Autumn/Winter 2022 show, with the designer.

Opposite: A look from Thom Browne's Autumn/Winter 2022 collection,
which was inspired by New York characters and individuality.

chapter 3

NEW YORK
SUBCULTURES

THE RiSE OF THE CiTY SUBCULTURE

Above all else, generation after generation of subcultures have defined and reinvigorated New York's fashion scene, rising from the underground ranks to mainstream culture. Subcultures first started appearing in New York City in a major way around the 1950s, bubbling up in opposition to the political and cultural mainstream. Not all of these countercultures had an effect on fashion, and not all of them were so intrinsically linked to New York City. The ones that were, however, were powerful in their undeniable aesthetic appeal.

In November 1952, an essay titled "This is the Beat Generation" was published in the *New York Times*. The beatnik was, loosely, anyone who rejected mainstream conventions and ideals in favour of artistic expression through spoken word, literature, music or visual arts. Allen Ginsberg, Jack Kerouac and William Burroughs were a few of the most famous beatniks, and Audrey Hepburn briefly played one in a scene in *Funny Face* (1957) at a jazz club. The look itself was one that put an emphasis on nonchalance – loose hair, baggy button-down shirts, striped black and white T-shirts, rolled-up jeans, skinny black cigarette jeans, black turtlenecks, dance leotards, bodysuits and kitten heels or bare feet. You could find beatniks all over Manhattan during the 1950s – a striking contrast to the uptight hair and

Audrey Hepburn in *Funny Face*, 1957, in a beatnik-style club.

Above: A beatnik inside a café, going barefoot, as was typical of the subculture.

Opposite: More beatniks gathering inside a dimly lit café.

feminine A-line dresses of the everyday conformists. Beatnik
men grew their hair longer and started wearing beards as
opposed to being clean-shaven, and beatnik women wore less
makeup and didn't get their hair permed – both signatures of
the mainstream. Interestingly, the all-black look of the New
Yorker has its roots deep in beatnik culture. Back then it said:
"I don't care to be like the rest of you." Now it hints at power
and offers an arresting conflict of visual identity: both "don't
look at me" and "look at me". The beatnik aesthetic was one
that would continue to be adopted by would-be intellectuals
even decades later – from berets to glasses.

But let's go back even further into the world of New York
subcultures. Counter to the beatnik, prep culture permeated
New York City on a different social level. It would also leave
a wake of style influences that would be copied for decades,
and adopted by New York designers like Ralph Lauren.

New York Subcultures

The prep is perhaps the oldest American subculture and it has major roots in New York City. In the early 1900s, an uptight, structured aesthetic known as "preppy" was born. Unsurprisingly, it got its name from how students at the top Ivy League schools, as well as the most elite prep schools, were dressing. The story goes that *Life* magazine sent a journalist to Vassar College (located in Poughkeepsie, New York, a few hours away from the city), then one of the wealthiest schools in the nation. The article revealed what the female students at Vassar wore: tweed skirts and Brooks Brothers' sweaters, polos and jeans. In response, Macy's launched an ad campaign based on the article, with the promise that it was possible to purchase every single item there. And so, the commodification of prep was born.

The upper crust of society in New York has mirrored elements of the prep wardrobe ever since. Indeed, some of the oldest brands that defined prep style in the early 2000s were born in New York City. Take, for example, Brooks Brothers, the oldest apparel brand in continuous operation in America. It was founded by Henry Sands Brooks and originally opened as H. & D. H. Brooks & Co in 1818, on the corner of Catherine and Cherry streets in Manhattan. It was renamed Brooks Brothers in 1850, after being taken over by his four sons. Brooks Brothers was initially known for the invention of the ready-to-wear suit, but it also produced the structured shirts, sweaters and skirts worn by prep students for generations. In the 1950s, the prep look became even more mainstream as women donned polo shirts and tennis skirts for organized sports. On a larger scale, celebrities embodied the prep look, including the actress Grace Kelly, who lived at the white-brick Manhattan House at 200 E. 66th St in the early 1950s, and who wore twinset sweaters, polos and silk neckties.

Actress Oona O'Neill, wearing a preppy look, 1942.
She married Charlie Chaplin one year later.

New York Subcultures

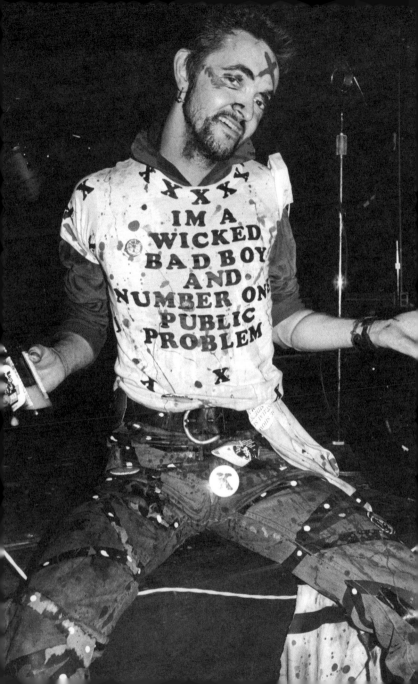

SUBVERSiON OF SUBCULTURE

Another extremely iconic subculture that has undoubtedly impacted New York City's fashion culture is punk. Following the very first countercultural movements of the 1950s, and the political protests and style explorations of the 1960s, the 1970s welcomed a new era of self-expression through fashion. Saint Mark's Place was home to many of the punks of the time; it also served as a welcoming place for beatniks in the 1950s and hippies in the late 1960s.

One gathering place for the punk subculture was Max's Kansas City, a nightclub and restaurant at 213 Park Avenue South. Performer Richard Hell, who was in several early punk bands, including Neon Boys, Television, the Heartbreakers and, later, Richard Hell & the Voidoids, often hung out there. He wore his own ripped-up T-shirts with dramatic slogans like "Please Kill Me". Above all else, an element of destruction was the hallmark of the punk's style: many of the performers wore ripped-up jeans and shirts, all exercises in DIY. They would also pin safety pins to shirts and hats. CBGB on the Bowery offered up another meeting place for punks and their fans when it opened in 1973.

The Ramones, Lou Reed and the New York Dolls were just a few of the popular acts behind the scene, which was inextricably tied to music. One of the defining staples of the punks was denim. Look at any punk band and you'll see it in all of its forms: jeans, jackets, skirts, and more. The New York Dolls famously wore children's jean jackets for an extreme,

New York Subcultures

An example of early punk style.

More examples of early punk style subcultures in New York City.

shrunken look. Debbie Harry of Blondie wore lots of denim jackets. The Ramones were known for their love of Levi's.

Many credit punk culture to London, and it did sort of happen in both cities simultaneously; there were overlapping political and economic issues, and the music spoke to both in each location. But the story goes that the original "PUNK" fanzine was published in New York City by cartoonist John Holmstrom, publisher Ged Dunn and local punk Legs McNeil in 1975. They were credited with popularizing the term "punk rock" (coined earlier in the decade by rock critics). Malcolm McLaren was in New York managing the New York Dolls during this time, and reportedly was so inspired by the original New York punk scene that he brought his own interpretation back to London. The SEX clothing shop he ran with his then partner, Vivienne Westwood, began selling ripped-up T-shirts threaded with safety pins.

B-boys of the 1970s created a subculture of their own.

At the same time in very different circles, the b-boys of the 1970s were creating a subculture of their own, and clothing was equally as important. The people who were b-boying (not the same thing as breakdancing – as they would tell you back then) were contributing to the wider conversation happening in hip-hop culture. This specific style and activity rose out of the Bronx, which was experiencing extreme poverty in the 1970s. Breaking, DJing and graffiti were intertwined.

Like the punks or beatniks, the b-boys represented an act of subversive rebellion, this time against the heavy disco subculture at the time. Many credit the style of their dancing to Latino culture, with mambo-inspired takes on modern breakdancing. The early b-boys served as a countercultural movement and used their dancing and dressing as a means of self-expression. One of the most famous b-boys was Anthony G. "Cholly Rock" Horne (born

The b-boys represented an act of subversive rebellion and took their style and moves to the streets and subways.

24 May 1960), who was introduced to the subculture in 1974 and originally started dancing at parties hosted by the Father of Hip Hop, DJ Kool Herc.

It wasn't uncommon for b-boys to wear sweatshirts marked with the colours of their group and the name of their crew. They also favoured Converse, tracksuits, knitted skull caps, loose Lee jeans and Pumas. When hip-hop became more mainstream, many elements of style of the original b-boys of the Bronx were reinterpreted.

Music continued to have an influence on subculture in New York, especially into the late 1970s. The subculture of disco spawned an entire era of fashion that would be talked about for ages. It also opened up the scene for more diversity in terms of race and sexuality. In Manhattan, Studio 54 was the arbiter of social status as icons like Grace Jones and Andy Warhol transcended art, culture and fashion to create a new vision of nightlife. On the dancefloor, these subcultures would later lead to even more diverse movements, like New York Ballroom culture, which embraced queerness.

In the late 1980s, as hip-hop had become mainstream, a certain Brooklyn subculture brought high fashion to the entire genre of hip-hop, laying out the blueprint of fashion in music as we know it today. Known as Lo Lifes, they were founded when two groups merged: Ralphie's Kids from Crown Heights, and Polo U.S.A. from Brownsville. Lo Lifes were specifically obsessed with the sporty, preppy culture of Ralph Lauren Polo, and would go to department stores around the city and walk away with these specific Ralph Lauren items. They would then wear each piece like a trophy, and incorporate references about the colourful shirts into

New York performer Grace Jones, who influenced music and style with her eccentric fashion.

New York Subcultures

Andy Warhol transcended art, culture and
fashion to create a new vision of nightlife.

New York Subcultures

their songs. What they did changed the relationship between
fashion and music forever, as well as the interpretations of
cross-cultural references. Here was Ralph Lauren, an iconic
New York designer who had built his entire aesthetic on
the idea of the upper-middle class prep, and there were Lo
Lifes, who took the idea and turned it on its head, making it
casual streetwear. They would also resell pieces in their own
community to redistribute the clothing, democratizing the
prep aesthetic in the process.

Lo Lifes were specifically obsessed with the sporty, preppy culture of Ralph Lauren Polo. Pictured are Lo-Lifes Naughty 40, Bek Live, Uncle Disco, and Big Vic Lo in 1988, dressed up to watch *A Nightmare on Elm Street 4: The Dream Master*.

CLUB ICONS

The club culture of the 1990s brought on an entirely new aesthetic and subculture that felt fresh. Teenagers and young people went to clubs including the infamous Limelight, to express themselves in ways that may have felt impossible during the day. There, under the hazy lights with the blaring music, they remade themselves as otherworldly characters. They decked themselves out in makeup, made their own costumes out of found objects, and documented it all on instant cameras. Walt Cassidy was perhaps one of the most iconic characters in the scene, and today he works as an artist in New York City.

What was unique about the New York City Club Kids culture was that it picked up on the many subcultures of the past and present. There were people who took inspiration from punk or hip-hop, but there were also those who went all out with gothic, head-to-toe black, complete with makeup to match. Many of the Kids went out nightly, and created entirely different characters, complete with new makeup, new hair and new costumes to impress their peers. Theirs was a subculture that valued dressing up more than anything else, as well as inclusivity and individuality. You could be anyone you wanted to be on the dance floor. The short-lived Club USA was the place to be seen and attracted people who followed high fashion. It featured a slide hanging over the dance floor and rooms designed by the fashion designers Jean Paul Gaultier and Thierry Mugler.

New York Subcultures

Iconic Club Kid Jenny Talia (also known as Jenny Dembrow) at Tunnel, 1993, photographed by Steve Eicher.

Opposite: The Club Kids scene valued individuality and people would often create new costumes for each event.

Above: New York City Club Kids culture picked up on the many subcultures of the past and present to create new identities.

"It wasn't until the mid 2000s that new subcultures fully emerged, like athleisure and its various tangents such as health goth."

The early 2000s in New York had little to no new subcultures, but there were some that reinterpreted subcultures of the past. McBling, for instance, melded the newly instituted Y2K aesthetic with hip-hop. It wasn't until the mid 2000s that new subcultures fully emerged, like athleisure and its various tangents such as health goth, which is a dark and minimal approach to wearing workout clothes in the everyday. TikTok gave rise to new trends in the 2020s, like cottagecore and dark academia, both of which draw from previous aesthetics like Lolita or gothic. Though these more modern subcultures are less directly tied to New York City than the rising subcultures of the past, it's impossible to walk through the city and not see their predecessors' influence.

New York Subcultures

A$AP Rocky in a normcore meets gorpcore look.

chapter 4

SOCIETY iN THE CiTY

For as long as New York City has existed, the epicentre of style has been connected to society and celebrity. Some of New York's earliest and most influential fashion moments happened at celebrity balls and galas, when people dressed to the nines to impress guests and make a statement.

One of the most memorable balls of all time, which would change the inner social circles of New York's elite forever, was the Vanderbilt Ball. Hosted in the spring of 1883, Alva Vanderbilt positioned the ball as the housewarming party for her newly built mansion, designed in the style of a French château by Richard Morris Hunt, at 660 Fifth Avenue in Manhattan. The theme of the party was historically accurate costumes, and people went all out: Mrs. Cornelius Vanderbilt II dressed as an "Electric Light" with a light-up torch, powered by batteries hidden in her dress. Miss Kate Fearing Strong wore a cat costume consisting of a taxidermized cat's head and seven cats' tails sewn onto her skirt. Alva's sister-in-law dressed as a hornet, with an imported headdress made of diamonds.

The society ball will always have an impact on New York style. Another famous example is the novelist Truman Capote's Black and White Ball, in which he invited 540 of his closest friends on 28 November 1966. Obviously, everyone wore black and white, and society's elite, like Norman Mailer, and William and Babe Paley, attended.

New York Style Icons

Lee Radziwill at Truman Capote's Black and White Ball, 1966.

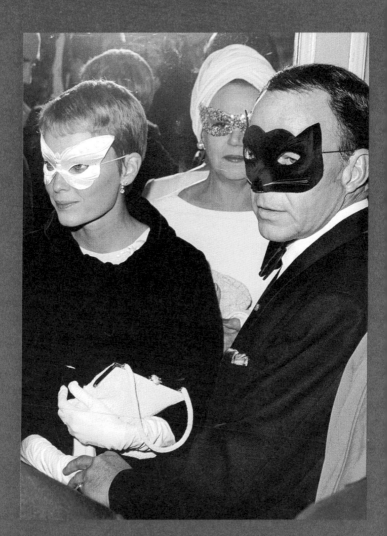

Above: Mia Farrow and Frank Sinatra at Truman Capote's Black and White Ball, 1966.

Opposite: New York style icon Jackie O, known for wearing pillbox hats, headscarves, oversized sunglasses, opera gloves, pearls and more, wearing a casual look while followed by famous paparazzi photographer Ron Galella.

The wealthy residents of New York City have always showcased their assets, motives and even politics through dress. Perhaps one of the best examples of this is another iconic New Yorker: Jackie O. Born in 1929 in Southampton to a well-off family, Jacqueline Lee Bouvier always had an interest in dressing up. From 1961 to 1963, she served as First Lady of the United States, the wife of President John F. Kennedy – and became an international fashion icon.

Jackie O wore trends, and the world watched and copied. A few of the most important and timeless icons this New Yorker brought to fashion's lexicon include the pillbox hat, the headscarf, oversized sunglasses, opera gloves, pearls, pea coats and capes, and all-white looks for summer. Many of the

New York Style Icons

accessories she wore would become wardrobe staples – like the oversized sunglasses, for instance, that celebrities hide behind even today. Just take a look at Audrey Hepburn's little black dress, opera gloves, sunglasses and pearls in the 1961 movie *Breakfast at Tiffany's*.

Though she plays a fictional New Yorker, the similarities between her look and what would later be Jackie O's look are striking. The dress was created by designer Hubert de Givenchy, who often dressed Jackie (even before she became First Lady in 1961).

The 1960s in New York City was also a time of experimentation in fashion for socialites, and what they wore often dominated headlines – much more so than is true today. Even though New York City felt progressive compared to many other places in the world during the 1960s, there were still rules, and they were mind-boggling. And the people who broke those rules were icons. Socialite Nan Kempner, who referred to herself as a clotheshorse, was famously denied access to the restaurant La Côte Basque in 1968 because she was wearing a pantsuit rather than a dress or skirt. This wasn't too out of the norm – many of the uptown restaurants wouldn't let women in if they were wearing pants in the late 1960s and early 1970s. Kempner removed her trousers and entered the restaurant wearing only her Yves Saint Laurent tunic.

Socialite Nan Kempner, who was famously denied access to the restaurant La Côte Basque in 1968, because she was wearing a pantsuit rather than a dress or skirt.

THE PERFORMERS

Many of the icons who also defined their style in the city of New York come from the world of performance, of course.

Screen siren Lauren Bacall was one of the most well-remembered style icons of the 1940s and 50s. Born in 1924 in the Bronx to a working-class family, Bacall was immersed in the world of fashion before she became an actress. She started out modelling for fashion magazines and her appearance on the cover of *Harper's Bazaar* led directly to her role in *To Have and Have Not* (1944) with Humphrey Bogart, whom she would later marry. In the early days of her career, she was known for oozing simplicity with a hint of masculine minimalism. She was also forward-thinking and was one of the first celebrities to wear true vintage on the red carpet: at the Oscars in 1979, she donned a vintage Delphos gown by Mariano Fortuny from the 1920s. Her style was celebrated in 2014 with an exhibition hosted by the Fashion Institute of Technology. She epitomized the ease and wearability of clothing – something New Yorkers carefully consider before they walk out of the door.

"Lauren Bacall epitomized the ease and wearability of clothing."

New York Style Icons

Actress Lauren Bacall, the New York style icon who got her start as a model.

"Denim jackets, faded band T-shirts, animal prints, berets, leather jackets and sequins took inspiration from punk subcultures."

The 1970s in New York brought forward a whole new group of fashion tastemakers in music. Perhaps one of the most memorable was Debbie Harry, lead singer of Blondie. In 1974, she co-founded the group in New York City. She defined an entire era of female punk rockers, not just with her clothing but also with her makeup and hair: shocks of platinum locks and bold, aggressively bright pink lipstick. Her denim jackets, faded band T-shirts, animal prints, berets, leather jackets and sequins took inspiration from the punk subcultures on the streets downtown, particularly in Saint Mark's Place where punk thrived.

Around the same time, Donna Summer was a New York style icon beckoning in the era of disco. She was often dubbed "Queen of Disco". She started her career in the 1960s as a singer in a band named Crow, influenced by counterculture movements in New York City. By the 1970s, she was well-known globally. Her sense of style was influenced by and connected to the infamous New York City club Studio 54, and there she mingled with designers like Halston and wore his slinky jersey dresses.

By the time the 1980s came around, Madonna had come to switch up the music scene and change the way the female musical artist was perceived forever. Moving to New York

Debbie Harry, lead singer of Blondie, was known for her punkish sense of style.

New York Style Icons

Donna Summer, an icon of New York style in the era of disco.

Madonna, who remains an influential style tastemaker even today.

City in 1978, she rose to fame with her debut studio album *Madonna*, released in 1983. She famously pushed boundaries and shocked people with her music, and she did the same with her clothing choices. In her video for 'Like A Virgin', she wore a wedding dress and the now famous "Boy Toy" belt. During her Blond Ambition World Tour in 1990, she commissioned Jean Paul Gaultier to design her extreme outfits: cone bras and golden leotards. She channelled Marilyn Monroe on more than one occasion, and went topless at a 1992 Jean Paul Gaultier show. Madonna's eccentricity and concept of strategically linking extreme fashion to performance would go on to influence other New Yorkers in the industry. Lady Gaga and Nicki Minaj have both worn jaw-dropping outfits and curated their own versions of

New York Style Icons

Above: New Yorker Nicki Minaj at the Met Gala.

Opposite: New Yorker Lady Gaga at the Met Gala, who has become famous for delivering over-the-top surprises with her outfits.

shocking style: at the 2010 MTV Video Music Awards Lady Gaga infamously wore a meat dress, while Trinidadian-born Nicki Minaj always delivers over-the-top surprises at the Met Gala, from Barbie pink bejewelled gowns that match her hair, to red sequinned dresses and veils dripping with crosses.

THE ECCENTRICS

Some might call this type of New York style icon eccentric, and that's not entirely wrong. New York has always embraced difference and diversity; iconoclasts have lived unconventional lives for decades in the city. Famed fashion editor Diana Vreeland was one of them.

Born in Paris, she moved to New York City, where her family were quickly welcomed into the circles of high society. She worked at *Harper's Bazaar* from 1936 to 1962 as columnist and editor, joining *Vogue* as editor-in-chief from 1963 until 1971. Vreeland was known to express herself through her clothing: she often wore extremely voluminous silhouettes, curled her hair into a distinct bob, wore bold red lipstick and bold, sculptural jewellery. The same sensibility was conveyed in her New York home, with an all-red living room and a royal blue floral bedroom.

Iris Apfel is someone from the same generation who has established herself as an oddball New York fashionista. At more than 100 years old, she can often be seen layering prints, colours and extreme, chunky jewellery with her signature rounded glasses. She started her career in textiles and has been a fixture of the fashion world, and the focus of its admiration, ever since. In 2005, the Metropolitan Museum of Art in New York presented an exhibition about Apfel, titled *Rara Avis (Rare Bird): The Irreverent Iris Apfel*. Giorgio Armani and Karl Lagerfeld attended, and Apfel has been the subject of many brand collaborations since.

New York Style Icons

The legendary Diana Vreeland in her all-red living room.

Above: Patti Smith at the Chelsea Hotel, 1971.

Opposite: Iris Apfel sits for a portrait during her 100th
Birthday Party at Central Park Tower in 2021.

On the more minimal side of the eccentric New York City
style icons, we have Patti Smith, the musician, author and
poet often called the "punk poet laureate". She exemplified
1970s New York and the rejection of gender ideals, opting
for button-down shirts, ties, blazers and oversized coats
with flat boots. She lived at the infamous Chelsea Hotel
with photographer Robert Mapplethorpe and often wore
his clothes.

New York Style Icons

THE iT-CROWD

New York City would be nothing without its perceived cool kids. Whether they made their names in the club scene or were scouted on the street, the underground it-crowd has its own rich history.

Grace Jones may be the original example of this. The Jamaican model, singer and actress began her modelling career in New York before taking off for Paris in the 1970s. In the early days of her career, she could be spotted in clubs in New York and Paris and became known for her striking bone structure, bold makeup and androgynous way of dressing. She was photographed by the top photographers, including Helmut Newton and Guy Bourdin. She perfected the look of sharp tailored suits contrasted with soft, flowing hoods, created by draping designs by Halston and Alaïa over her head. Likewise, Bianca Jagger was a fixture at Studio 54 and became a New York style icon of a different type via her wedding to Mick Jagger. Like Jones, she pushed the boundaries of gender when it came to dressing, and was married in a slick, tailored white wedding suit by Yves Saint Laurent. On the club scene, she wore splashy red sequinned dresses with matching berets.

New York Style Icons

Opposite top: Grace Jones, known for her striking bone structure, bold make-up and androgynous way of dressing.

Opposite below: Bianca Jagger at Studio 54.

"The interesting thing about this city is that it will change the way you dress, no matter who you are."

In 1994, actress Chloë Sevigny became *the* It girl of New York when *The New Yorker* devoted an entire feature to her. She had just come off starring in a Sonic Youth video filmed in Marc Jacobs' showroom, modelled for the trendy (now-defunct) brand X-Girl, and had a shoot in *Details* by Larry Clark, who also cast her in his new movie, *Kids*. Back then, she wore sequinned Betsey Johnson dresses with tiger striped tights, and today, she is still regarded as one of the most influential of New York style icons. In 2022, she got married in three different looks by Jean Paul Gaultier couture by Glenn Martens, Loewe by Jonathan Anderson and Mugler by Casey Cadwallader.

The kind of fascination people held for Sevigny has been repeated over and over again, as other It girls appear. Today, the concept of the It girl feels less monumental as social media has made the style icons we admire more accessible and attainable. However, the It girls of the past still maintain their intrigue.

New York Style Icons

Actress Chloë Sevigny outside a fashion show.

Perhaps one of the most iconic of those in recent years are Mary-Kate and Ashley Olsen (who now have their own luxury fashion brand, The Row, which typically shows at Fashion Week.) In their New York reign in the mid 2000s as NYU students, they harnessed the look of the bag lady: all-black and messy but (in their case) expensive. Their style was one that was replicated by hordes of models between fashion shows and well documented on fashion blogs at the time. What made their looks especially interesting was the unlikely but discerning element of practicality.

The modern iterations of New York's it-crowd today come from all different aesthetics. The actress and model Julia Fox, who has become a New York style personality, can often be seen at Lower East Side hangouts and is well-documented in her all-black, gothic dominatrix looks. Model Bella Hadid, who spends much of her time in New York City, has popularized the revival of the Y2K aesthetic and puts a big emphasis on wearing designer vintage.

The interesting thing about this city is that it will change the way you dress, no matter who you are.

New York Style Icons

New York style duo Mary-Kate and Ashley Olsen.

chapter 5

NEW YORK WARDROBE STAPLES

So, you want to dress like a New Yorker? The one defining element of New York style is an openness and willingness to wear anything and be free of judgement. Walk down any of the streets in any neighbourhood, and you can easily see an eclectic mix of different styles from casual to formal, minimal to maximal, high-end to low-end. Still, there are a few keys of New York style that nearly every city dweller has in their closet.

Colourful, printed coats of all lengths and shapes

New York is notorious for its cold, harsh winters. In fact, during the winter, and because most New Yorkers don't have cars and use public transportation, you'll find most of them covered up, head to toe. During these times, the only thing you'll see is your coat, so many who love fashion focus on choosing a vibrant, statement coat in some sort of unusual colour or print. New Yorkers also wear a lot of black puffer coats for practicality, but the people who love style really lean into the idea of the coat as the total look. Many opt for vintage, floor-length options (no one else will be wearing the same look as you), printed trench coats with expressive buttons, and even colourful puffers with quirky prints.

The author mixing and matching prints with a colourful coat.

Fashion-forward blazers, oversized, form-fitting, and printed

The blazer is another well-worn essential in the New Yorker's wardrobe, partly because it offers so much versatility. In Soho, you'll see people out and about shopping wearing a cool oversized blazer in a bright colour, or a simple menswear-inspired fabric thrown over a vintage band T-shirt with baggy jeans. But uptown, you might see more structured versions of the blazer worn in the form of skirt suits and more structured options. The great thing about the blazer is that it works year-round in New York. You can wear an oversized printed blazer in the summer with a miniskirt, but you can also wear an oversized blazer in the fall or winter with a hoodie layered underneath it and a coat or jacket layered on top of it. The value of the blazer is that it effortlessly fits into every New Yorker's aesthetic, from sporty streetwear to prep and maximalist.

New York Wardrobe Staples

An example of a printed blazer, a necessity for New York fashion.

Jeans

Much like the blazer is a versatile staple of every New Yorker's wardrobe, so too are jeans. While New York dresses up substantially more than the rest of the country, jeans are used as a means of self-expression – and can be worn by all the different style tribes in different ways. You'll often see jeans worn in offices, even the offices of conventional finance, but you'll see them at Fashion Week too. A few denim staples that are more specific to the modern New Yorker: black, straight-leg jeans, which can be worn with anything from an oversized blazer to a button-down shirt, baggy and low-slung jeans, which are worn in the summer with corsets, crop tops and sweaters; and straight-leg jeans of various washes, worn with vintage T-shirts or, for those who embrace a more eccentric look, layered under dresses and skirts.

Denim done different ways is always a welcome
addition to any New York wardrobe.

Telfar Bags

It's nearly impossible to spend a day in New York City and not see someone carrying a Telfar bag. Born in Queens, Telfar Clemens founded his eponymous label in 2005 as a student at Pace University and launched the classic shopping bag, which now comes in multiple sizes and colourways. The bag itself is a simple tote with the circular Telfar logo and can be carried with its shorter handles or worn crossbody. Celebrities such as Solange, Selena Gomez and A$AP Ferg have all been seen wearing the bag. And while Paris may be defined by Chanel and Hermes, New York has embraced local, young, affordable designers and made Telfar a staple of its style DNA because the brand represents inclusivity in everything it does. Many have since referred to the bag as the "Bushwick Birkin", as the brand embraces queer, BIPOC culture and is often seen all over Brooklyn. The larger style of the bag fits a laptop and more – essential for New Yorkers on the go.

Opposite: An example of the Telfar shopping bag.

Above: Seen at Fashion Week, a limited-edition UGG x Telfar bag paired with a Christopher John Rogers dress.

New York Wardrobe Staples

Sneakers

If there's one thing to know about New York City, it's that you'll be walking a lot. No other city has embraced sneakers quite like New York. The majority of the people who live here walk everywhere and commute by train, bus or even ferry, all of which aren't the most friendly towards heels or stilettos. Sneakers have become the unofficial shoe of the New Yorker, and you'll often see more formal pieces like dresses, suiting, and tailored separates styled down with Nike Dunks, Air Jordans, running shoes or designer sneakers from labels like Chanel. Vans, in particular, are seen just as often with jeans as they are with a full designer look. In fact, you'll probably see more locals wearing sneakers than heels at New York Fashion Week. The benefits are, of course, that you can walk everywhere and still cultivate your own aesthetic.

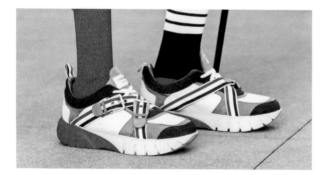

Above: You'll probably see more fashion industry insiders wearing sneakers than heels at Fashion Week.

Opposite: A Fashion Week attendee pairs a colourful coat and printed jeans with Vans.

New York Wardrobe Staples

Baseball caps

Another element in the mix of New York style is the baseball cap. Consider it all-American or dressed-down, but New Yorkers wear them on coffee runs or when walking their dogs first thing in the morning because it's such an easy way to hide unstyled hair. It also borrows from New York's popular paparazzi culture; you'll see lots of celebs wearing the humble baseball cap, sometimes with a pair of sunglasses, to disguise themselves. But locals also wear the cap and the fashion crowd tends to wear them in ironic ways, styled with feminine dresses or with oversized blazers and tailored shorts. A few classic styles to try are the signature New York Yankees caps, or one with your favourite designer's logo, from big names like Celine to smaller indie brands like Batsheva, who typically hand out branded ball caps to guests at Fashion Week. If you want to go in a more ironic direction, choose a vintage one, or an unexpected ball cap from your favourite restaurant like the iconic Odeon where a coveted pen is also a New York showpiece. The more obscure the hat, the better.

New York Wardrobe Staples

A Fashion Week guest pairs a baseball cap with her outfit for the ultimate high-low styling move.

Leather jackets

The leather jacket is another New York staple that is ubiquitous, especially in the spring and autumn, when weather can fluctuate drastically from day to night and week to week. Long considered a wardrobe icon, the leather jacket can toughen up any look. The classic look is definitively black, but you'll also see people experimenting with eccentric colours like red or pink, and even with prints ranging from zebra and leopard to floral or studded. The reason why this jacket has become so popular in New York City lies in the garment's roots. Like many New York staples, practicality is important, and many leather jackets were initially designed for jobs in the military and aviation fields. Indeed, the first moto leather jacket that we know of in modern history is associated with New York: in 1928, Irving Schott designed the first leather motorcycle jacket and sold it for $5.50 at a Harley-Davidson store in Long Island. Schott makes leather jackets to this day.

The leather jacket remains an essential item of the New York wardrobe.

All-black

For almost as long as people can remember, an all-black wardrobe has been associated with New York. That's partly because a slew of iconic New Yorkers across culture made it their look, from Jackson Pollock to Laurie Anderson and Lou Reed. But the all-black look has also been associated with various subcultures that have influenced the lexicon of New York style, from beatniks and punks to goths and new wave club kids. Black has been promoted as the colour that is flattering for all, no matter who you are. But for New Yorkers, wearing all black is also about conveying a sense of power and stature while, at the same time, blending in. In Western culture, the hue was initially reserved for mourning until the fifteenth century, when it became associated with Philip the Good, Duke of Burgundy. At the time, the colour was considered luxurious because it was more expensive. Today black is probably the only colour you can do literally anything in, and that's why New Yorkers, both past and present, love it.

New York Wardrobe Staples

An all-black look seen at Fashion Week, with just a hint of colour coming from the accessories.

chapter 6

THE RISING TALENT

As a city, New York has one of the most diverse examples of fashion culture. Nowhere else can you walk from one neighbourhood to another, or even down a different street, and see such a varying display of sartorial oddities. In New York, style tribes thrive, but you can also be as individualistic as you want with the way you dress.

That's part of the reason why New York City has become the de facto place for emerging designers to strike out on their own and find success. In Milan or Paris, you might get to discover a few new names at major exhibitions, sitting alongside the big houses, such as Chanel, Dior and Prada, but New York's show calendar is truly dominated by emerging brands. These designers come from all over the world to display in the city. You can also walk down the street and see all kinds of people wearing pieces from young designers – like Telfar bags – and that's unique to New York.

A few emerging brands to make bigger names for themselves in the past few years are Vaquera, Pyer Moss and Eckhaus Latta. Though these brands are entirely different aesthetically, what they have in common is the community they've built and the cult following they've achieved. Vaquera, founded in 2013 by Patric DiCaprio, Bryn Taubensee, David Moses and Claire Sullivan, gained wide support for their work, which the brand itself calls "fashion fan fiction". Playing with the idea of subversion,

A look from a Vaquera runway show which took place on a street downtown, in which models ran down the middle of the road.

the label has created outfits made of American flags and trash bags (pieces decidedly designed to mirror memes), while oversized T-shirts printed with lingerie and massively proportioned ruffle dresses have massive appeal to fashion insiders and editors. Vaquera partnered with Dover Street Market (founded and owned by Rei Kawakubo of Comme des Garçons) to receive funding and production support and, as a result, started showing at Paris Fashion Week in 2022.

Likewise, Pyer Moss has found success as a Black-owned brand that showcases fashion with a strong point of view. The label, founded by Kerby Jean-Raymond in 2013, has a history of putting political views on display through artful performances during its runway shows, such as using a choir to showcase the effects of police brutality in America during the Spring 2016 season. Pyer Moss has since collaborated with Reebok on capsule collections.

Eckhaus Latta has been around since 2011, founded by Mike Eckhaus and Zoe Latta. It developed its cult following by creating gender-inclusive knits, denim and raw-edge logo T-shirts on street-casted models of all shapes, ages and genders.

Perhaps one of the biggest reasons why New York is so welcoming to new designers is the rich history of the Garment District. Beyond that, New York is also home to the greatest fashion schools in the country. Many of the city's top designers went to school here and these schools have been the first choices on the preferred list to attend for new names and emerging talents. The Fashion Institute of Technology was founded in 1944 – when the fashion industry in New York

Pyer Moss's first couture show took place at Villa Lewaro in Irvington, New York, at the estate of America's first female self-made millionaire, Madam C.J. Walker, who, when she died, was the wealthiest self-made Black woman in the US.

Parsons School of Design is considered the city's
most prestigious school for fashion design.

City was just starting to take shape in a major way. It was a
technical school to prepare young people to work in fashion,
and there were originally just about 100 students. FIT focused
on putting people as close to the real industry as possible, and
by 1959, it had relocated to a nine-storey building on Seventh
Avenue, right in the heart of the Garment District. What's
quite unique about the school is that it is a public college,
meaning it's more affordable, so competition for entry is
tough. Today, FIT offers programmes ranging from advertising
and photography to cosmetics. Some of the city's most iconic
designers are also alumni, including Calvin Klein, Norma
Kamali and Michael Kors.

Dennis Basso

The Museum at FIT showcases a variety of revolving fashion exhibitions that are open to the public.

Parsons School of Design is another famous fashion school, founded by American Impressionist William Merritt Chase in 1896. In 1904, arts educator Frank Alvah Parsons came on board, eventually becoming the director of the school and launching programmes that had never been seen before in the country. In fact, Parsons was the first school in America to offer a degree in fashion design in 1904 (then called Costume Design). Like FIT, Parsons today offers fashion degrees that span across management, photography and art. It also has its fair share of famous alumni, including Anna Sui, Donna Karan, Marc Jacobs and Tom Ford.

SHOPPING

When it comes to shopping, there's certainly no shortage of it. New York has some of the most epic department stores in the world, with tons of history too. Take, for example, Macy's, which began as a small dry goods company in 1858, on the corner of 14th Street and 6th Avenue.

In 1902, Macy's moved to Herald Square, where it remains today. The store is the largest department store in the United States, and one of the largest in the world, at 230,000 m² (2.5 million square feet). It is a must-see for its sheer size alone. Head uptown by about 20 blocks, and you'll find a department store heaven: with Saks Fifth Avenue, Bloomingdale's and Bergdorf Goodman all close to each other, each with very different vibes, but all equally worth a visit.

Not far from Macy's is Dover Street Market, the retail store founded and owned by Comme des Garçons creator Rei Kawakubo. Encompassing seven floors and a basement, it stocks some of the most high-fashion items in the country. Fresh from the runway are pieces from brands like Thom Browne, Simone Rocha, Gucci and Maison Margiela, and you'll also find streetwear from Vans and Supreme, plus a focus on emerging designers. The Supreme section of the store is always busy and draws a crowd, as does the standalone Supreme store in Soho, which has some of the longest lines of any retail store in New York when there's a new drop.

The shopping scene of the city has a decidedly varied feel in different neighbourhoods, but in the most simplistic sense, uptown is ruled by department stores and luxury boutiques

New York Fashion Today

Dover Street Market, founded and owned by Comme des Garçons creator
Rei Kawakubo, is known for a mix of high-end and emerging luxury designers.

lining the street, where downtown is more concerned with
mixed boutiques that feel a bit younger or stores that hinge
on the more unconventional.

As vintage shopping has become more mainstream and
popularized, the city's second-hand shops have become
all the more crowded. New Yorkers have always visited

Above: Beacon's Closet is one of the best spots in
the city to shop secondhand fashion.

Opposite: The department stores in midtown put on a
full production show for holiday windows.

second-hand shops like Beacon's Closet, which has locations
throughout Manhattan and in Brooklyn, and L Train Vintage
in Brooklyn. There's nothing like the thrill of finding
something you never knew you wanted, and the prices
are great for gently used designer goods and true vintage
items. New Yorkers have also put more of a focus on the
sustainability that shopping second-hand offers – they realize
the power behind their dollar.

New York Fashion Today

THE EVENTS

One of the things that makes the culture of New York fashion so unique is the society that surrounds it all. The first Monday in May marks the most talked-about fashion event in the world: the Met Gala.

Originally established in 1948 by fashion publicist Eleanor Lambert, the event is a fundraiser for the Costume Institute of the Metropolitan Museum of Art and also serves as the annual opening of its biggest fashion-themed exhibit of the year. It's the most prestigious event in fashion, as celebrities, A-listers and fashion industry insiders come together and dress up for the evening's chosen theme.

It's one of the most talked-about fashion events because of the experimentation that comes with it: while celebrities tend to play it safe at the Oscars and other galas, the Met Gala remains a forum for self-expression and experimentation. The boldest dressers, like Rihanna or Lady Gaga, make their choice of outfit an act of performance art, often opting for outfits that shock and surprise. Other regulars, like Sarah Jessica Parker, are notorious for sticking to the theme to the extreme. Other celebrities and A-list actors have become ones to watch at the event over the years, such as Blake Lively, who has opted for dramatic Versace gowns with swanning tails. They dress carefully, paying close attention to the accessories, shoes and nails; Lively even opted for a New York skyline manicure by Elle Gerstein for the recent New York Gilded Age theme.

Anna Wintour at the Met Gala.

"While celebrities play it safe at the Oscars, the Met Gala remains a forum for self-expression."

For many years, the Met Gala was largely known as an industry high society event, but after 1995, and following the involvement of Anna Wintour, the editor-in-chief of *Vogue*, it exploded in popularity and began to make headlines. Since then, the legendary editor has made the event a household name and the first of its kind for relevance. She controls everything, down to the most minute detail, from the guest list to the ingredients in every single item on the menu.

The other most talked-about event is, of course, New York Fashion Week itself, which happens twice a year, once in spring and once in autumn. The entire fashion community comes together to organize a calendar full of shows and events showcasing the newest collections. While the emerging designers have taken over the spotlight in recent seasons, many of the biggest names in American fashion still host shows or events for buyers, editors, writers and industry insiders. Anna Sui, Coach, Carolina Herrera, Tory Burch and Proenza Schouler are a few of the regulars who typically show during NYFW. New York designers who made their business in the city don't always show in New York and sometimes end up decamping to Paris. But for some, it's worth it to come back for special occasions, like when Thom Browne presented his Autumn/Winter 2022 show in New York City after seasons abroad in Paris, pegged to the exhibition at the Met's Costume Institute, *In America: An Anthology of Fashion.*

New York Fashion Today

Blake Lively at the Met Gala wearing a gown inspired by the Statue of Liberty.

Above: The final walk of Thom Browne's Autumn/
Winter 2022 show inspired by New York.

Opposite: Ralph Lauren's show at the Museum of
Modern Art during New York Fashion Week.

THE LOOK

Street Style in New York is like a competitive sport, especially during Fashion Week. There's no shortage of peacocking, and all the major magazines in the country typically have their own photographers on the scene to take pictures of the most interesting examples of real-life dressing outside the shows. There's a street style scene in every city, more specifically in the four main cities that host the biggest fashion weeks (New York, London, Milan, Paris), but New York stands out in more than a few ways.

Unlike the more traditional European cities where there's not as much variety or diversity in the style, New York has a massive range, due in part to its intrinsically eclectic and diverse selection of people living in the city and working in the industry. In Paris, you might see several people with the same aesthetic; in Milan, many of the street-style stars reflect the Italian heritage or aesthetic. In New York, you'll see a beautiful slew of contradictions at every show: people wearing sweatpants, ballgowns, upcycled sets with DIY doodles; people donning head-to-toe designer looks for the brand whose show they're attending, others opting for affordable fashion from Zara, T-shirts, jeans, or athleisure-inspired looks. You're guaranteed to see it all. Some of the New York street style photographers have become celebrity names in their own right. While we may not have the original Bill Cunningham anymore, the most-watched street style photographer in the industry is probably Phil Oh, *Vogue*'s

New York Fashion Today

A Fashion Week attendee wearing denim-on-denim and loafers.

YouTuber and content creator Ashley Rous outside a fashion show.

Actress Jordan Alexander on the streets of New York.

"You can walk down any street and see a range of personal style which is truly enlightening."

go-to photographer who began his blog, Street Peeper, in the mid-2000s and documented people around the world with interesting style. He was eventually brought on to Vogue.com to shoot Fashion Week street style globally, and is known for his own style of mixed prints. He has an eye for interesting details and arresting sartorial flair, and shoots all the names to know as well as intriguing passers-by.

That's the thing about New York: you can walk down any street and see a range of personal style which is truly enlightening. People push the boundaries here: there's pink hair, shaved heads, bold eye makeup, tattoos and fashion that conquers the status quo. New York fashion embraces all today, and that's what makes it so exciting.

New York Fashion Today

Opposite: Stylist Gabriella Karefa-Johnson, one of the most-watched street style stars in the New York scene, known for her maximalist approach to getting dressed.

Overleaf: A group of friends attend New York Fashion Week and experiment with colour and silhouette.

iNDEX

CREDITS

The publishers would like to thank the following sources for their kind permission to reproduce the pictures in this book.

Alamy: Patrick Batchelder 142; Robert K. Chin – Storefronts 143; Everett Collection 8-9; Historic Collection 39; Patti McConville 141; Maximum Film 24; Newscom 27; Photo 12 47; PictureLux/The Hollywood Archiv 67

© **Victor "Thirstin Howl The 3rd" DeJesus:** 81

© **James Ewing Photography:** 138

Ricky Flores: 76-77

Getty Images: Neilson Barnard 103; Edward Berthelot 117, 121, 124, 155; Bettmann 7, 10, 35, 36, 41, 68, 69, 70, 90, 92, 109b; Randy Brooke 57; Timothy A. Clary 54-55; Dia Dipasupil 18; Sean Drakes 60; Steve Eichner 82, 84; The Estate of David Gahr 107; Noam Galai 106; Ron Galella 93, 109t; Rose Hartman 49, 78; Heritage Images 42; Taylor Hill 149; Arturo Holmes 62, 135; Images Press 51, 53; JNI/Star Max 111; Melodie Jeng 123, 127; Dimitrios Kambouris

102; Rob Kim 112; Jeff Kravitz 145; John Lamparski 58, 59; Harry Langdon 100; Fernando Leon 139; Jamie McCarthy 63, 146; Michael Ochs Archives 75; Jeremy Moeller 131,152; Cindy Ord 136; Jose Perez/Bauer-Griffin 21b, 153; Mark Peterson 85; Robin Platzer 80; Eileen Polk 74; Michael Putland 101; Ebet Roberts 72; Roy Rochlin 118; Silver Screen Collection 97; Michael Stewart 16; Christian Vierig 86; Victor Virgile 22-23; Chris Walter 98; Angela Weiss 148; Donell Woodson 156-157; Daniel Zuchnik 122, 125, 150

Shutterstock: Berry Berenson/Condé Nast 45; Andrew Eccles/Cw Network/ Kobal 21t; Arthur Elgort/Condé Nast 48, 52; Horst P Horst/Condé Nast 32, 33, 105; Duane Michals/Condé Nast 46; Alex Oliveira 15; John Rawlings/Condé Nast 37; Richard Rutledge/Condé Nast 30; Francesco Scavullo/Condé Nast 95

Every effort has been made to acknowledge correctly and contact the source and/or copyright holder of each picture and Welbeck Publishing apologises for any unintentional errors or omissions, which will be corrected in future editions of this book.

Credits